HOW TO MAKE A Picture Book

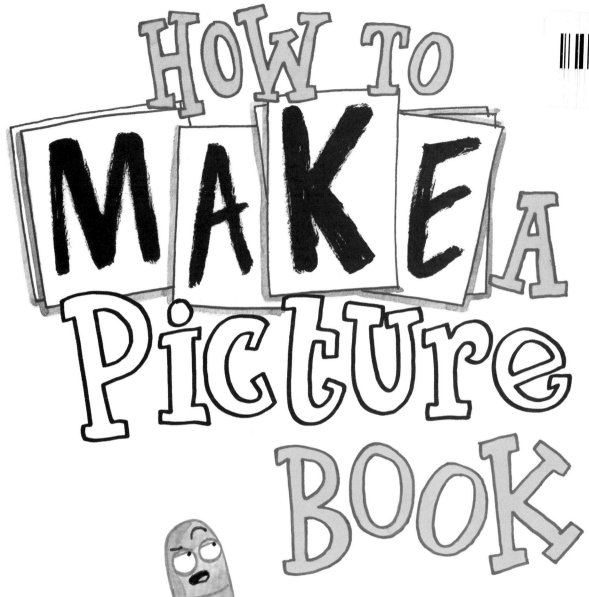

Dr. Elys Dolan
(Talented author and illustrator)

And also Bert!

Oh look, a title. That's very professional . . . Hang on! Who let Bert put his name there?

Hi. I'm Elys Dolan and I write the words and make the pictures for children's books.

Of course, I'm not really a worm. I'm just appearing as one because it's quicker to draw than a person. You see, time is of the essence.

WE NEED STORIES AND WE NEED THEM NOW!

And I'm relying on YOU to make them. So, I'm going to show you how to make picture books, like I do.

A picture book is a book that uses words, pictures, and page turns to tell the story!

Yes, thank you, Bert. He's my "assistant." So, writing words AND making pictures are going to be very important.

I'm going to show you, step by step, how to make your own picture book. You just need to follow the instructions and try out the activities.

Who doesn't love activities?

I love them!

That's enough, Bert.

Now grab your pens and pencils and let's get making!

IDEAS

The first thing you need when making a picture book is an idea for what the story will be about.

But sometimes having a good idea for a story isn't easy, even if you try really hard.

LOOK!
So tricky!

So I want to show you where I go when I'm stuck for ideas. This means I need to take you somewhere very special.

BEHOLD! My . . .

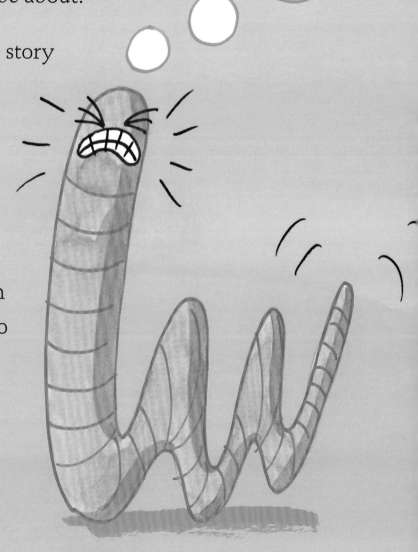

GALLERY OF MUSES

These are all my favorite things! I love villains and detectives and bears and doughnuts, guinea pigs in armor, when chickens do literally anything, and most of all . . . PAPER CLIPS!

Just magnificent.

I think you guys at home need your own gallery of muses. What's the time? It's . . .

ACTIVITY TIME

ACTIVITY TIME! WOO!
Why don't you try drawing or writing some of your favorite things? Look! I've drawn mine.

You like some varied things, Bert.

Now that we know that Bert loves wrenches and fried eggs, let's move on. Next we can use our favorite things to make a story idea. It's time to do some . . .

STORY MATH*

It's easy. Just take two of your favorite things and add them together to make a story idea. Let's try it with two of Bert's favorite things:

Really big dinosaurs   plus . . .   Pizza!   equals . . .

*Contains no real math.

Let's try some more:

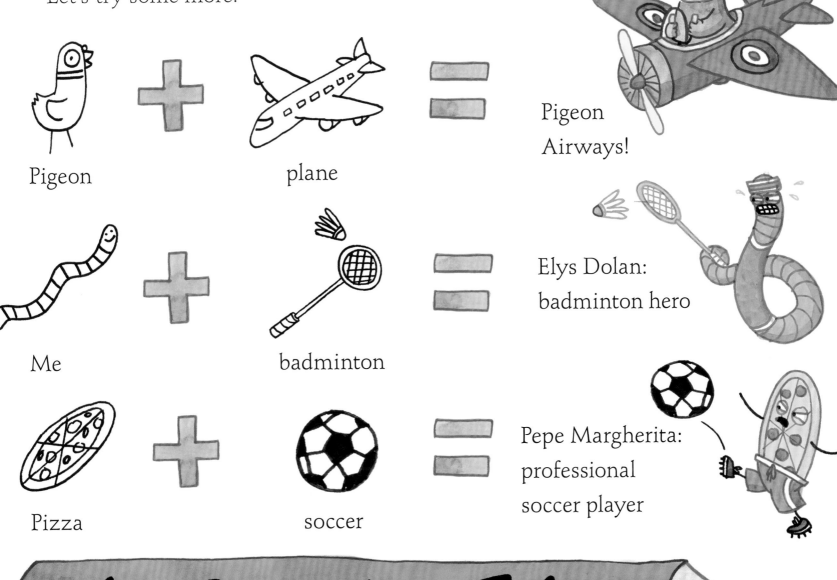

Pigeon + plane = Pigeon Airways!

Me + badminton = Elys Dolan: badminton hero

Pizza + soccer = Pepe Margherita: professional soccer player

ACTIVITY TIME

It's time to make your story idea. Take some of the things you drew earlier, and do a bit of story math. Add them together, just like we did, and see what story ideas you get.

CHARACTERS

Now that you've got a story idea, I think you're ready to learn about characters.

Character

Characters are the people in your story. They're like your actors!

Yes, Bert, I was getting to that. Now, your characters
don't have to be humans. They could be . . .

An animal! Like
this pig in a hat.

Good day.

Or even a thing, which we
call an inanimate object,
like these fruit friends!

I also have a hat!

So, Bert, you need to choose the
main character for your story idea.

Umm . . .

PIZZA DELIVERY DINOSAUR!

Look, Elys, I've finished my character! Elys!

Hi!

No, Bert! Characters are so much more than just how they look.

For them to work well in your story and be believable, we have to get to know them really well.

First, we need to find out how they behave. I do this by
drawing the character doing lots of different things.

Like doing a dance.

Or taking a shower.

Having lunch.

Or . . . doing this.

Solving crimes!

It was you!

Being a bit sad.

We're starting to understand a bit about our character's personality, but we still need to figure out what exactly is going on in their head. That means it's time to . . .

INTERVIEW OUR CHARACTER

Welcome to the show! Tonight I'm going to ask the most complex questions to really get to know this character. Brace yourselves, viewers—it's going to be heavy.

What's your name?

Marge.

WOW!

I love this show!

SETTING

Next we're going to talk about setting.
This is the place where the story happens.

WELCOME TO **BUG TOWN**

BAKERY

But what if the story happens here, in **THE WHITE SPACE?**

CAFÉ

Calm down, Centipede.
Yes, not all stories have a
setting that's a place. If they
don't, then the characters
have to work really hard.

But I don't like working hard, so our story is going to have a setting that is a place. To figure out a setting, I start by thinking about what my character's home would be like.

Do you know about homes, Bert?

Of course! Here's mine.

THE fancy STORE

Bert, do you live in a lemon, where you also grow lemons?

Yep!

That's so weird, Bert, so weird. But really, we should be thinking about our character's home, not your lemon house.

And to do that we're going to . . .

ZOOM OUT

OK, Bert. First, draw Marge's bedroom. Think about what things are in there and what they tell us about Marge's life.

What does her bedroom tell you she cares about?

Next, let's zoom out and see where her
room is. What is Marge's apartment like?

Good job, Bert! You learned that from the interview,
didn't you? You've also drawn someone else in
that shop. That must be who works with Marge.

Now let's zoom out even farther and see where the shop is.
What do you think it would be like to live in this town?

ACTIVITY TIME

It's your turn to draw your story's setting.

1. Draw your character's bedroom. What do the things in it say about them?

2. Draw the outside of their home. What do they live in? It doesn't have to be a house—it could be a castle, a submarine, or a huge lemon.

3. Draw the place where that home is. It could be anywhere, like a town, a forest, outer space, or under the sea.

Pizza?

Yes, please.

Now it's time to write a... **Story**

Now that we've got an idea, a character, and a setting, we need to decide what will happen in our picture book's story.

But stories are really hard! How am I supposed to know what should happen? I only know about lemons!

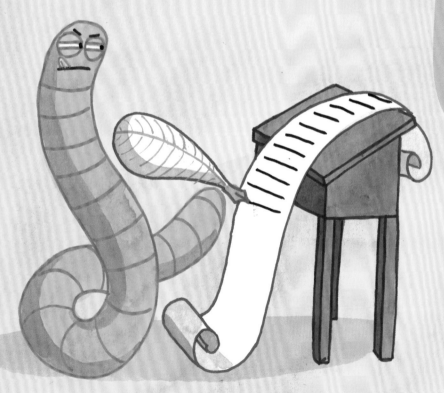

Get a hold of yourself, Bert. It's simple. You just need to be a . . .

Story Builder

Look! I even have a trowel.

I prefer wrenches.

Now, Bert, I have some simple building blocks that we can use to build a story. You just finish the sentences, draw a picture in each block, and voilà! Let me show you.

There once was . . .

Every day . . .

But then one day . . .

Because of that . . .

And because of that . . .

And finally . . .

So from now on . . .

There once was . . .

This first block is where you introduce your character and what they do.

. . . a dinosaur called Marge, who worked at Dino Pizza doing deliveries.

Every day . . .

. . . Mr. Marco made the pizzas. And Marge waited to deliver them.

In this next block you explain what your character's normal life is like. Come on, Bert, you can draw faster than that.

But then one day . . .

This is where something new or exciting happens. It should be different from your character's normal life.

. . . Mr. Marco was sick. Marge would have to make the pizza! And it happened to be the day of the town's pizza competition.

Because of that . . .

. . . Marge struggled all night to make pizza, but she just couldn't make them the right shape.

Next, you show how your character reacts to the new thing. What do they do? How do they feel about it?

And because of that . . .

Stories have a domino effect, with each event causing another. Here, show what your character's reaction causes to happen next.

. . . Marge entered the Pizza Showdown, but it didn't go very well.

And finally . . .

. . . Marge was so upset that she stomped all over her kitchen. And she made a discovery.

huh?

SQUISH!

We're nearly at the end. Here you show how your character might fix things. Do they get what they want or not?

So from now on . . .

This block is your ending. Here you show what your character's life is like now. How has it changed from the beginning?

. . . Marge's dino-shaped pizzas were a hit! Marge was the new Dino Pizza chef.

DINO PIZZA

STOMP STOMP

SOLD OUT!

ACTIVITY TIME

THERE ONCE WAS...

EVERY DAY...

BUT THEN ONE DAY...

BECAUSE OF THAT...

AND BECAUSE OF THAT...

AND FINALLY ...

I made a story! And if I can do it, you can too. Try drawing your own set of story blocks. Then finish the sentences and draw a picture for each of them using your own story idea.

BERT'S BONUS

How to Make a Picture Book

Psst! It's me, Bert. Now that you know what's going to happen in your story, you're going to need a book to put it all in. While Elys is not looking, I thought I'd show you how to make your own book, made of paper and everything.

1 Measure how tall and wide you want a single page of your book to be.

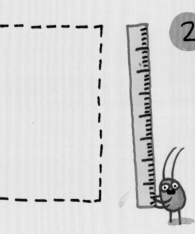

2 Double how wide it is so it's two pages next to each other.

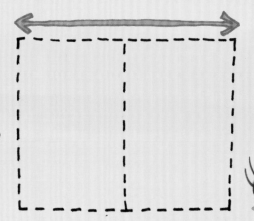

3 Cut out one shape of that double-page size for every 4 pages you need.

So if your book will have 32 pages, you need to cut out 8.

SNIP!

4 Fold each of those shapes in half.

5 Put them in a neat pile, ready to be bound together. There's a few ways you can do this.

6 You could tie a string tightly around the middle where the fold is.

7 Or you could stitch the middle with a needle and thread, but you'll need grown-up help.

8 Or you could staple where the fold is.

And look! You've got a book to put your story in. You can even draw a picture on the front and back to make a cover. Why don't you have a go at making your own before it's time for the next step?

USING PAGES

What have you been up to, Bert? Growing more lemons?

Er, yep! I definitely wasn't showing everyone how to make books.

Good, that's my job. So now that you've built your story, it's time to write and draw it into a book. First, decide how many pages your story needs.

Picture books usually have 32 pages. How many pages do you want your book to have, Bert?

10,000,000!

That's too many.

Hang on a sec, everyone, I'm hungry. I'm going to order a pizza.

Done!

You already know that in picture books both the words and pictures tell the story, so every page is going to need a picture and probably also some words. The challenge is deciding what those pictures should look like and how the words and pictures should use the space on the pages.

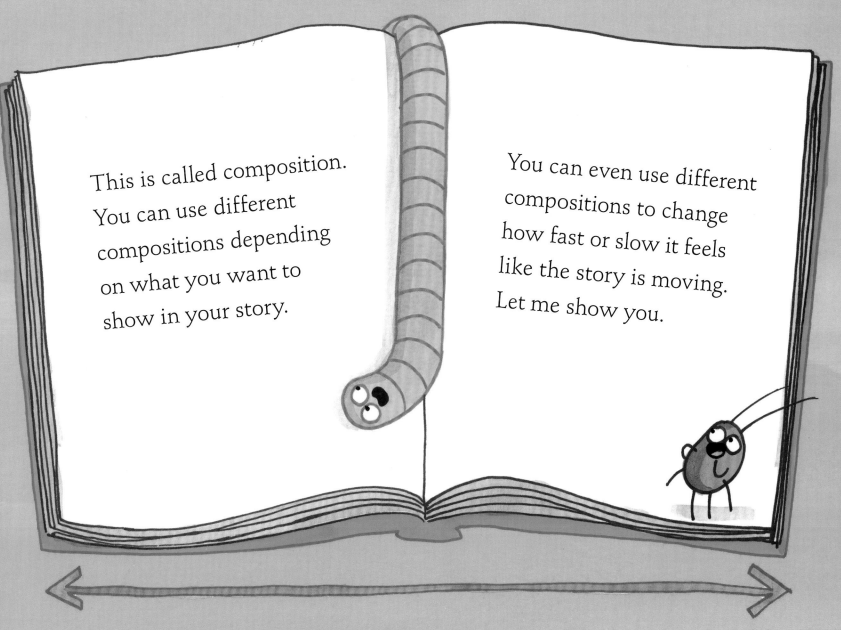

This is called composition. You can use different compositions depending on what you want to show in your story.

You can even use different compositions to change how fast or slow it feels like the story is moving. Let me show you.

(Two pages next to each other like this are called a double-page spread.)

Marge was out delivering pizzas, just like she did every day. But what Marge didn't know was that this was going to be her trickiest delivery yet.

THE POOL

BAKERY

CAFÉ

Did someone order a pizza?

ICE CREAM

Yes, Elys did, but the road is blocked! You'd better find a way through quickly, or Elys will be HANGRY!

For example, you can use both pages together, like this, to show one big picture with lots of details.

THE fancy STORE

WORM TOWER

BUSINESS BANANA

Park

This is good for introducing where your story is happening. It also makes it feel like a slow bit of the story, because the reader spends lots of time looking at all the details.

But then, if you change the composition and zoom in, it can make a moment in the story feel dramatic and important, because we're focused closely on just one thing.

Marge wasn't about to let that happen!

If you put a picture in a frame like this, it makes the reader feel further away from the action and it can make whatever is going on inside feel more contained. It's also a useful way of separating the words from the pictures if you don't want them together.

If you want to show action, like a chase or a fight, you can use lots of little pictures, called vignettes, on one page. This shows lots of moments without using much space, which makes it feel like it's a fast bit of the story.

Marge leapt onto the ice cream van,

ran across the roofs,

slid down the banana,

bounced off the leaf,

hopped across the bees,

and dived to deliver the pizza.

 Bert, why are you describing everything that's happening in the pictures?

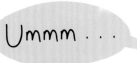 Ummm . . .

You don't want the words to repeat what we can already see in the pictures. The pictures should tell us something that the words don't say, and the words should tell us something that we can't already see. Have another try, Bert.

Marge knew that with the roads blocked, she'd have to take to the skies!

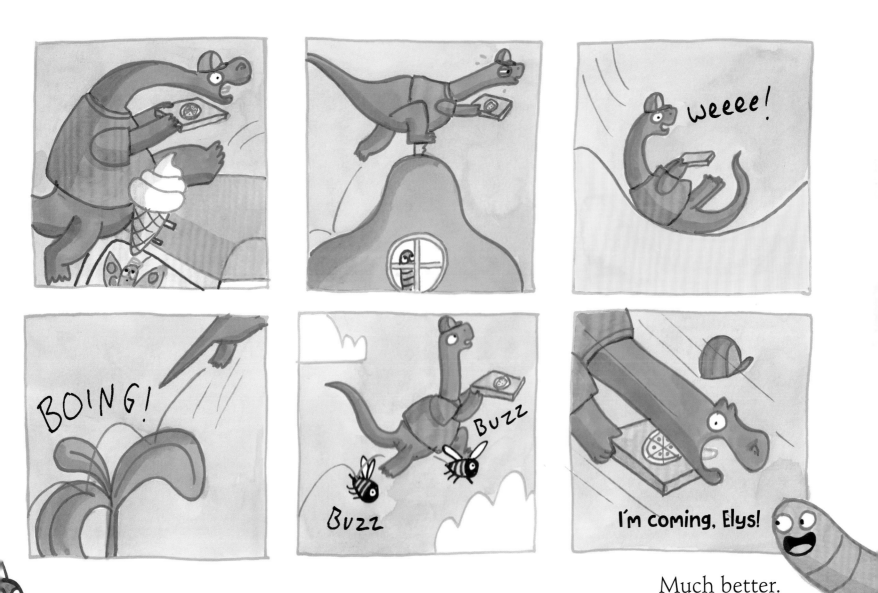

Much better.

Will Marge make it on time? A page turn like this can be used as a cliffhanger—a pause to make the story more exciting.

If you want a bit of your story to feel like an important moment or an ending, you can use two pages together, like this, and keep the image quite simple.

THUMPH!

ACTIVITY TIME

It's time for you to write and draw your story onto the pages of your book. Remember to change the compositions like Elys showed you, depending on what is happening on each page. Also, make sure your words tell us something different from what we can see in the pictures.

Oh look! My pizza.
Yummm, still warm.

Good work, you've nearly finished your picture book. There's just one last thing to talk about.

COLOR

Here's one last pro tip to help
you make your picture book perfect.
This is too advanced for Bert,
so he's not here.

Let's talk color.

You're probably going to want to color in
your pictures, which is great. Who doesn't
love color? My favorite is orange.

I like blue.

Did you hear something? Anyway, the colors you choose for your
book aren't just about making things look pretty. Different colors
make us feel different emotions or remind us of different
things. Let me tell you what these colors remind me of.

Blue: Sadness, the sea, Bert.

Red: Anger, fire.

Pink: Love, sugary things like cotton candy.

Green: Trees, nature, slime.

Black: Scary things, darkness, heaviness.

Yellow: Warmth, the sun, happiness.

When you're choosing the colors for your pictures, imagine what you want the reader to feel or to think about during that bit of the story. Choose the color that makes you feel that way.

Finally, we've reached the end of this book. And, even better, we've finished a brand-new book! I hope you're now ready to write and illustrate lots of your own picture books. I can't wait to read some of your stories.

So it's time to say goodbye from me, goodbye from Bert, and goodbye from everyone else too! Help yourself to a copy of *Dino Pizza* and one of Bert's complimentary lemons.

This is actually pretty good, Bert. Great job!

The End.

I'm going to go home,
put on my bathrobe, and
spend some quality time
with my paper clips.

I might start work
on my second book.
Pigeon Airways did
sound fun.